TABLE OF CONTENTS

SEA ANIMALS

AN INTRODUCTION FOR CHILDREN FROM 6 TO 10

Conception
Émilie BEAUMONT

Images
Lindsey SELLEY

Translation
Lara M. ANDAHAZY

FLEURUS

CETACEANS

There are two kinds of cetaceans: baleen whales (like the blue whale) and toothed whales (like sperm whales, killer whales and dolphins). Cetaceans are mammals; they give birth to live babies that they nurse. They all have a sort of nostril called blowhole on the top of their heads that they use to breathe. You can see the spouts of water they make when they breathe from far away. Cetaceans make noises. Some sounds let them find their way and locate prey, others are used to communicate among themselves.

Blue Whales

Blue whales can be up to 100 feet long and weigh more than 100 tons. They spend the summers in polar waters but prefer warmer waters in winter. Blue whales are generally alone or accompanied by their babies. They eat tons of krill (tiny shellfish that float in the water).

There she blows!

Blue whales are the largest of all living mammals on our planet.

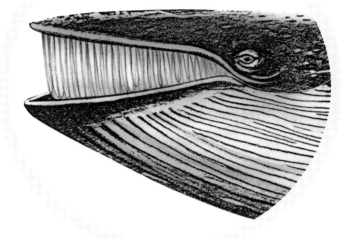

Killer Whales

Killer whales are formidable animals that move about rapidly. They are generally found in groups with one leader. Killer whales are about 20 feet long and weigh just over a ton. Their jaws have pointy teeth. They attack sea elephants and seals as well as other whales and dolphins and sometimes even fish such as tuna. They are very intelligent, are easily tamed and like humans.

Funny Teeth

The upper jaw of some whales is doted with very hard plates of whalebone called baleen. This acts like a filter to help them collect food. The plates are more or less close together depending on the size of the animals they eat.

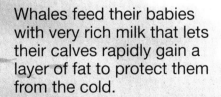

Whales feed their babies with very rich milk that lets their calves rapidly gain a layer of fat to protect them from the cold.

Sperm Whales

These cetaceans are easily recognizable by their large heads that make up almost one third of their bodies. Only their lower jaws have formidable teeth that can be up to almost 10 inches long. The largest sperm whales weigh about 45 tons. Sperm whales eat mostly squid. They are able to dive almost one mile down in order to catch giant squid! White sperm whales are very rare.

DOLPHINS

Dolphins are not fish, they are marine mammals. They belong to the same family as whales—cetaceans. They give birth to live babies that look like them. They have brains, hearts and lungs like we do. Dolphins are fantastic swimming machines between 6 and 30 feet long. They can swim for long periods of time at more than 18 miles per hour. They can even swim as fast as 45 miles per hour. Dolphins generally live to be about thirty years old.

Baby Dolphins

Dolphins generally mate in spring and their babies are born twelve months later. They nurse for nine months.

Dolphins have very soft skin. When you pet a dolphin, it feels like you are touching silk.

When baby dolphins are born, they come out tail first.

Dolphins perform beautiful water ballets made up of jumps out of the water and wonderful splashes.

Dolphin Calls

Dolphins communicate among themselves with a very complex "language" made up of clicks and whistles. By studying dolphins we have learned that some of the noises they make help them find their prey and orient themselves in the water.

Dolphins can have babies from the time they are eight years old. Baby dolphins' enemies are sharks.

Some types of dolphins live in fresh water. One of these is found in the Ganges River (in India). They have long snouts with lots of teeth (see the picture below). They are blind and eat the shrimp and fish that they find in the mud on the bottom of the river.

Men's Friends

Captive dolphins are very easy to tame. They can put on marvelous shows and give the impression that they are very happy to perform.
Their very powerful tails let them stand up on the water and even move backwards while standing up.

There are also white dolphins called belugas.

OCTOPUSES

Octopuses have been described by many famous authors as bloodthirsty monsters able to drag sailors to the bottom of the sea or kill divers. There really are giant octopuses but they are very rare. Most of the time these smart, soft-bodied animals are timid and run away at the first sign of danger. They are able to make their bodies long and thin in order to worm their way into narrow places as well as change shape and color in order to hide from their enemies.

Their Hide-outs

Octopuses generally live in holes that they protect by building a sort of wall made up of rocks and even bottles, old tires and other objects that they collect off the seabed.

Once in a Lifetime

Octopuses mate only once in their lives. After mating—which can last several hours—females lay eggs more or less quickly depending on the season and which species they belong to. They lay millions of eggs that they attach to the walls of their caves. Female octopuses watch over their eggs very carefully, so carefully in fact that they even forget to eat.

Fighting Moray Eels

Octopuses often fight with moray eels over holes to live in. Octopuses almost always lose to the moray eels' sharp teeth. Octopuses also fight among themselves by trying to strangle each other. The loser turns gray and then white before letting go. The winner turns bright red.

Defending Themselves

Octopuses have eight arms covered in suckers that they use to feel, recognize, grab and hang on to objects. Their mouths have sharp beaks.

Ink to Hide In

When octopuses feel threatened they eject a cloud of black ink that turns into a thick screen in a few seconds. They take advantage of this ink screen to swim quickly away without being seen by their enemies.

Octopuses generally live about three years. They usually live alone and eat mostly crabs and other shellfish. They particularly love rock lobsters! Their enemies are sharks, dolphins, sperm whales and above all, moray eels.

FISH

Fish have backbones and because of this belong to the large family of vertebrates. They move through the water by bending their bodies and tails. Their fins are used to keep their balance and change direction. Fish are covered with scales that protect their skins. Their scales come in different sizes and are more or less easily visible. Their bodies are covered by a thick, slimy liquid called mucus. Fish breathe by taking water in through their mouths and letting it out their gills (the slits you can see behind their eyes).

ray

Flat Fish (Rays)

Rays are flat fish that have eyes on the top of their heads and fins on their sides. They live at the bottom of the sea and hide under the sand at the slightest danger. Some rays are able to leap spectacularly out of the water.

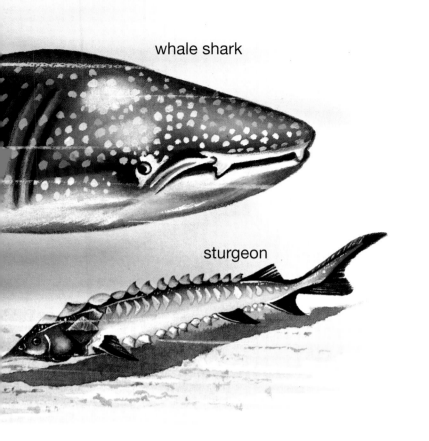
whale shark

sturgeon

Some Fish Can Fly!

Flying fish run away from their enemies by speeding towards the surface of the water. They shoot out of the water and fly over the waves for a few seconds. They use their fins like wings. Flying fish can go as fast as 45 miles per hour.

The biggest fish of all is the whale shark. They can be up to 65 feet long. They are the most gentle of all sharks. The smallest fish is less than half an inch long.

The fish that live the longest are the sturgeon. They can live up to 100 years compared to other fish that live between 5 and 20 years.

At first, baby fish don't look like adults.

Parrot Fish

The mouths of parrot fish end in hard, sharp beaks that they use to nibble away at coral to get at the algae and other microscopic animals that they eat. Before going to sleep they produce a cellophane-like substance and roll up in it for protection.

Fish lay eggs. Some fish lay their eggs in the sand or attach them to seaweed. Others let their eggs float in the water.

SALMON

Salmon are amazing fish. They are able move from salt water to fresh water and return to the exact river in which they were born several years later. These beautiful fish can get as big as six and a half feet long. Wild salmon are in danger because they need clean water to reproduce and rivers are becoming more and more polluted with waste from factories and sewers. Overfishing is also one of the reasons they have disappeared from certain areas.

Salmon undergo certain changes when they leave the ocean and go up river. They change color and the males' heads change shape. Their jaws change and a hooked beak appears.

What Bravery!

Salmon leave the ocean and return to the river in which they were born in order to reproduce. They are guided by their wonderful sense of smell which can identify the odors in their river. During this long voyage they go up waterfalls, struggle against the currents and jump over rapids.

After mating and laying eggs, salmon get old and die very quickly.

Laying Eggs

Female salmon lay their pretty, orange-colored eggs on the sand or gravel. They can lay up to two million eggs. Young salmon swim to the ocean when they are about two years old.

They can jump 6 feet high! In some rivers men have installed series of pools in steps called fish ladders to help them get over the bigger waterfalls. Few salmon make it to the end of their journey; many are injured and crash into rocks on the way.

Salmon Farms

In some parts of the world, people raise salmon in salmon farms. Salmon farms are generally built where rivers empty into the ocean. They are made of wooden tanks with nets in them. The tanks are filled with baby fish. The baby salmon are fed lots and lots of food to make them grow quickly!

SHARKS

When you first hear the word "shark" you often think of huge, terrifying monsters. It's true that they have a bad reputation, but out of 250 different species of sharks only 30 are dangerous. For example, the largest of all sharks, the whale shark, is harmless even if it can get as big as 65 feet long. It only eats microscopic animals.
On the other hand, 20-foot-long white sharks are dangerous—they have been nicknamed "man eaters."

Sharks—Greedy Feeders

Sharks feed at night most of the time. They love squid and any fish they can find. They even attack other sharks and whales. When they open their mouths to capture their prey, their lower jaw moves forward and the upper jaw lifts up. This way, their

Blue sharks are without a doubt the most handsome of all sharks because of their color and shape. They live alone most of the time and are dangerous. They can get to be up to 23 feet long. Their jaws are powerful weapons with seven rows of razor-sharp teeth.

gills

Sharks' Jaws

They have many teeth placed close together. When one of their teeth is destroyed another one grows back in eight days. Amazing, isn't it?!

Dolphins Attack Sharks

Dolphins form groups to attack sharks. They rush at them at high speeds and hit them in the ventral area (on the sides) or destroy their gills which kills the sharks.

mouths are positioned in front and not on the bottom of their heads. Sharks are attracted by blood and they can smell it a long way away. When they smell blood they rush in a frenzy towards the wounded animal and tear it to pieces. Sometimes sharks even swallow non-edible objects like chunks of wood and metal. What greedy-guts they are!

sawfish

hammerhead shark

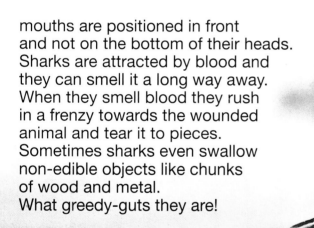

Funny Heads

Out of all the different species of sharks, two have very funny-shaped heads.
Hammerhead sharks—look at where his eyes are!
Sawfish—when these sharks see a school of fish they wave their sawlike noses around like swords and then gobble up the fish they wound and kill.

17

COMMON FISH

Look closely at these two pages and you will see fish whose names you probably know even if you don't recognize them. These fish are often the victims of overfishing done with huge nets that capture baby fish as well as adults and can cause certain species to become extinct. Did you know that more than 60 million fish are caught every year? That's quite a lot! There are about 20,000 different species of fish in the world that can be eaten.

angler fish

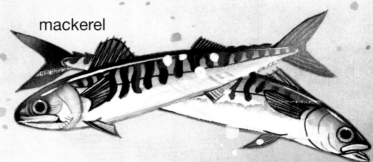

mackerel

Mackerel

Mackerel have black stripes on their backs and are often found in groups of several hundred fish called schools.

Cod

Cod are found in cold water and can lay up to ten million eggs! Cape Cod, in Massachusetts, was named after this fish because there were so many of them.

cod

sole

Turbot and Sole

These two fishes are flat and have eyes on the top of their heads. They are found at the bottom of the sea. They often hide in the sand. They move by waving their bodies.

turbot

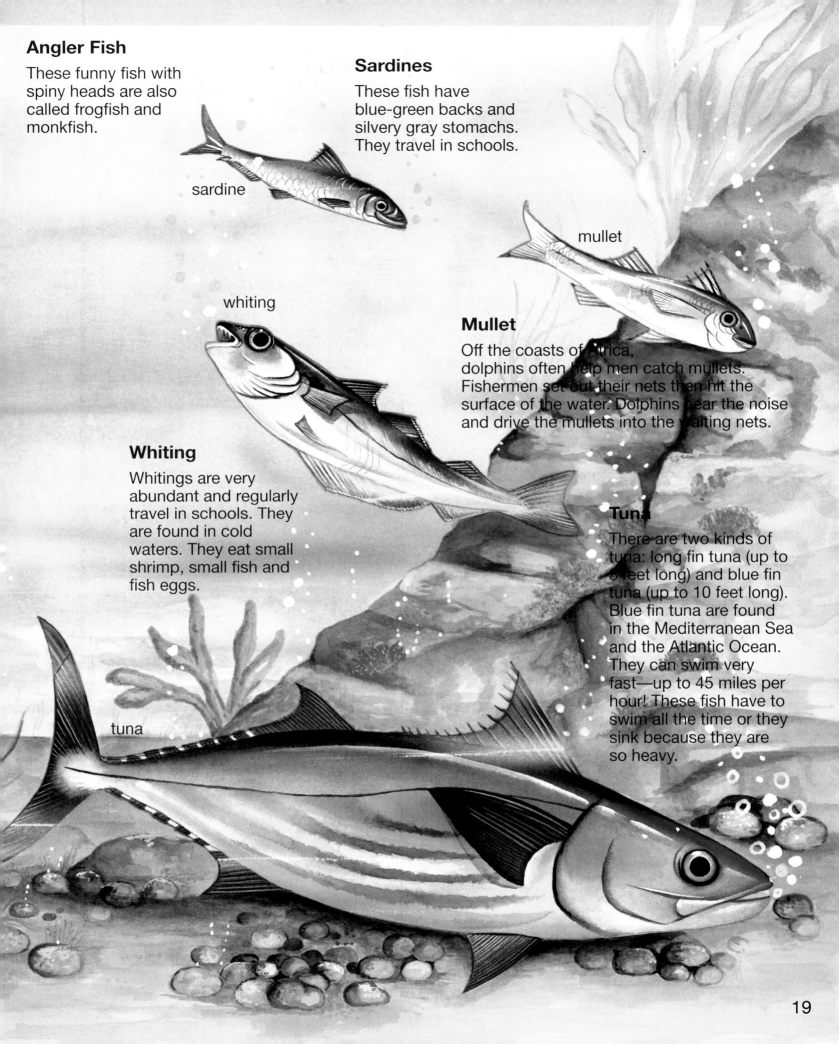

Angler Fish

These funny fish with spiny heads are also called frogfish and monkfish.

Sardines

These fish have blue-green backs and silvery gray stomachs. They travel in schools.

sardine

mullet

whiting

Mullet

Off the coasts of Africa, dolphins often help men catch mullets. Fishermen set out their nets then hit the surface of the water. Dolphins hear the noise and drive the mullets into the waiting nets.

Whiting

Whitings are very abundant and regularly travel in schools. They are found in cold waters. They eat small shrimp, small fish and fish eggs.

Tuna

There are two kinds of tuna: long fin tuna (up to 3 feet long) and blue fin tuna (up to 10 feet long). Blue fin tuna are found in the Mediterranean Sea and the Atlantic Ocean. They can swim very fast—up to 45 miles per hour! These fish have to swim all the time or they sink because they are so heavy.

tuna

19

ODD FISH

The undersea world is full of strange creatures.
Look closely at these two pages and you'll find a few odd fish. Some of them live in the deepest parts of the oceans where there is no light at all and others are found in tropical waters.

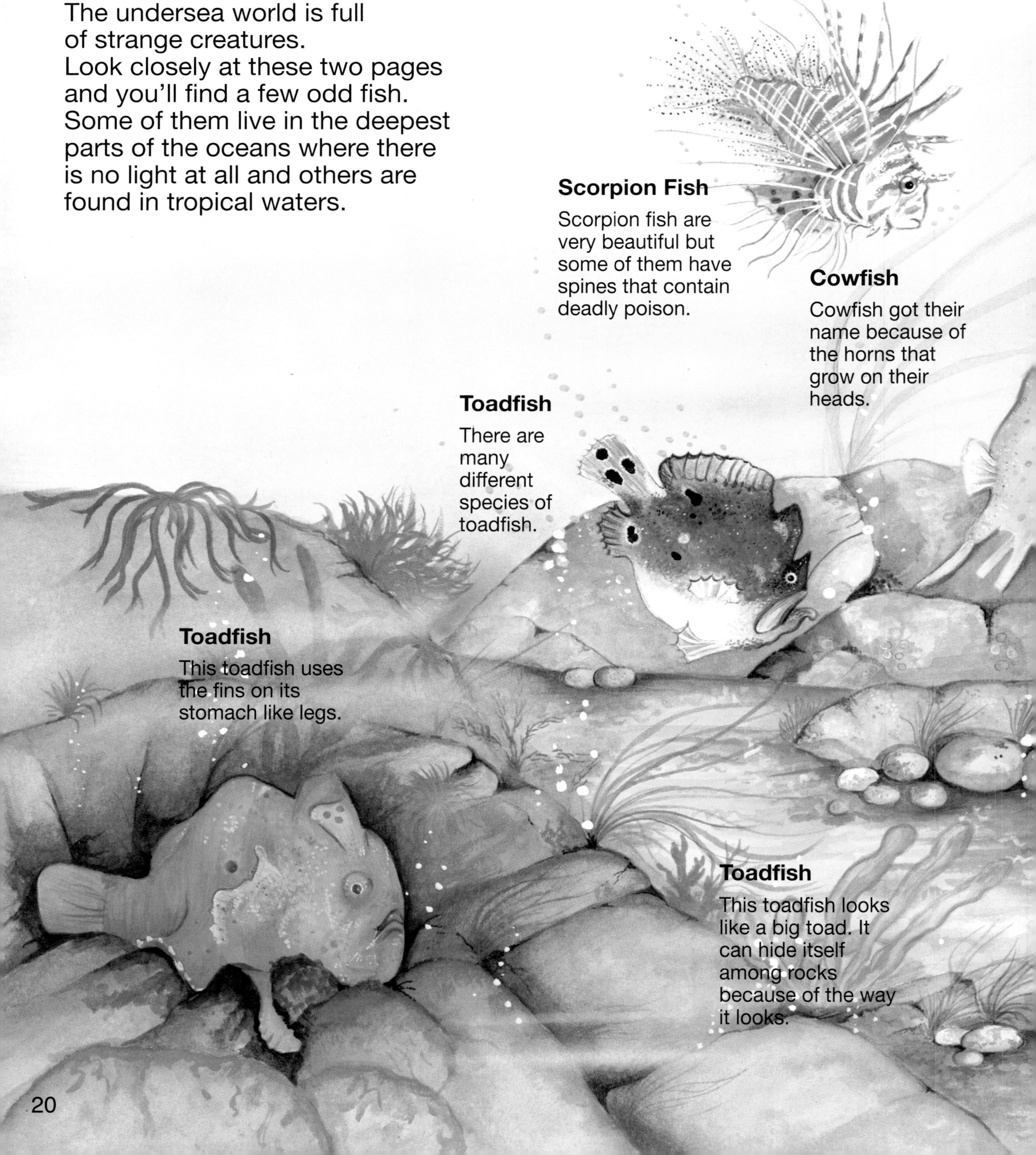

Scorpion Fish

Scorpion fish are very beautiful but some of them have spines that contain deadly poison.

Cowfish

Cowfish got their name because of the horns that grow on their heads.

Toadfish

There are many different species of toadfish.

Toadfish

This toadfish uses the fins on its stomach like legs.

Toadfish

This toadfish looks like a big toad. It can hide itself among rocks because of the way it looks.

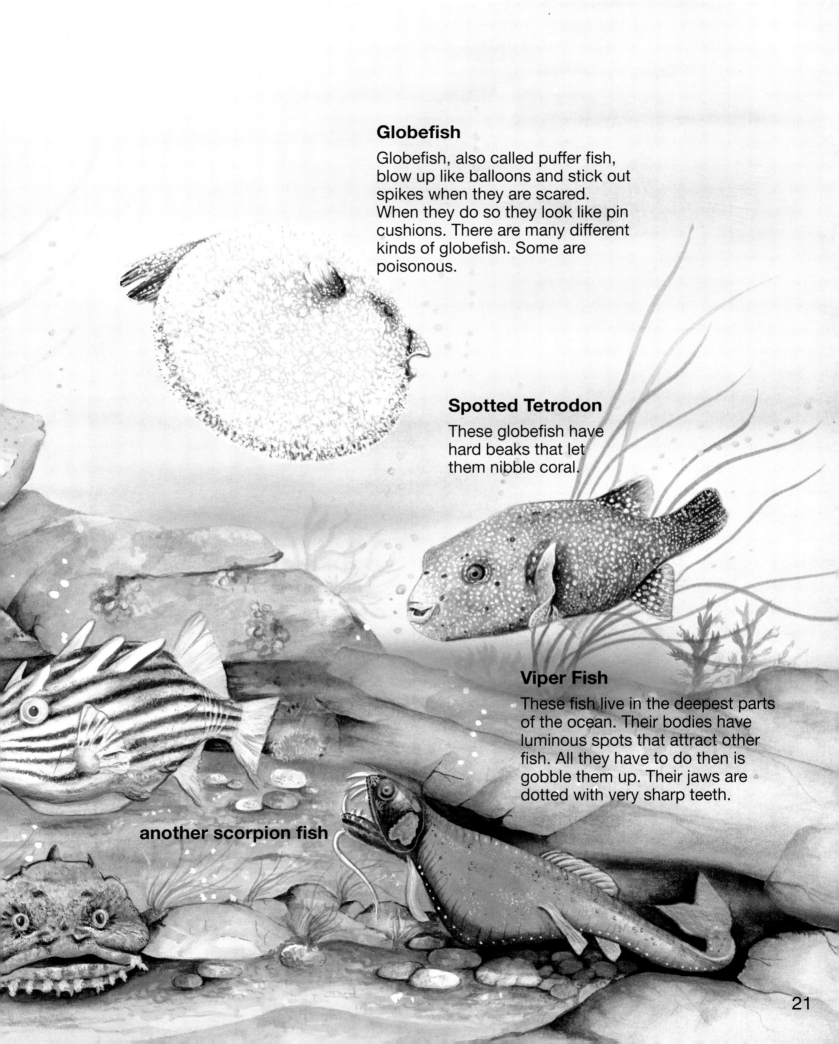

Globefish

Globefish, also called puffer fish, blow up like balloons and stick out spikes when they are scared. When they do so they look like pin cushions. There are many different kinds of globefish. Some are poisonous.

Spotted Tetrodon

These globefish have hard beaks that let them nibble coral.

Viper Fish

These fish live in the deepest parts of the ocean. Their bodies have luminous spots that attract other fish. All they have to do then is gobble them up. Their jaws are dotted with very sharp teeth.

another scorpion fish

21

CRUSTACEANS

Crustaceans (or shellfish) live in the rocks at the edges of beaches or at the bottom of the sea. As they grow bigger they have to shed their carapaces (shells) and grow bigger ones. For example, lobsters change shells about twenty times in five years. They are vulnerable after they shed their shells because their bodies are no longer protected. They hide in holes until their new shells get hard. Some crustaceans like the lobster eat their old shells.

The largest lobster ever found weighed 44 pounds and was over 3 feet long.

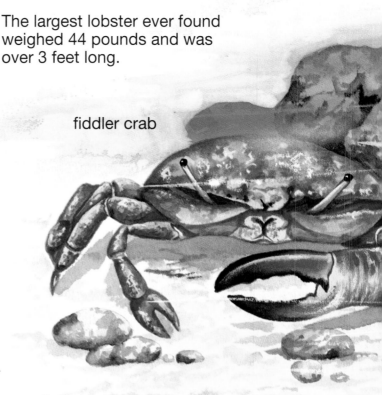

fiddler crab

Lobsters

Lobsters sometimes attack fish such as the moray eel when they are trapped between two rocks. They sometimes fight each other as well. Their claws are important when it is time to eat—the biggest is used to crush and grind food and the smallest has tiny pointy teeth used to tear apart the lobsters' prey.

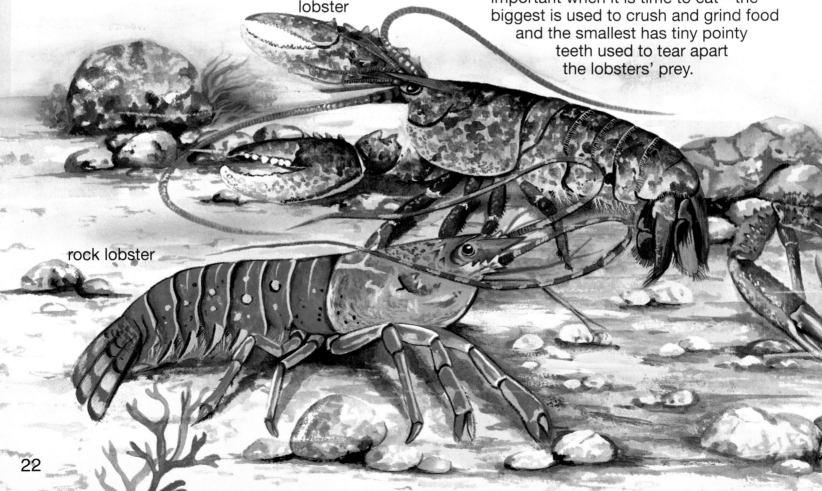

lobster

rock lobster

hermit crab

The tiny larvae that come out of crustaceans' eggs do not look like their parents. They have to undergo a number of changes before they become adults.

Crustaceans Lay Eggs

Shrimp, like all crustaceans, lay tiny eggs that they keep attached between their legs for close to six months until they hatch.

Rock lobsters, unlike regular lobsters, have small pincers. They have long sensitive antennae that help them sense their environment.
Spider crabs look a little like big stones which lets them hide.
Fiddler crabs have only one large claw that they wave around to attract females.
Hermit crabs don't have shells like the other crustaceans do. They live in empty shells abandoned by other animals.

spider crab

common crab

Safe and Snug

This minuscule crab has snuck into a mussel to escape its enemies. The mussel is glad it is there because the crab will eat up the bits of food that its host doesn't like.
Some crabs hide under the sand to keep away from their enemies while others hide in cracks in rocks or wrap themselves in seaweed.

23

MOLLUSKS

Mussels

Mussels live on rocks. They cling to them with the help of tiny stringlike filaments.

mussel

Scallops

Scallops lay around on the sand most of the time. When enemies come near they scamper away very fast. They move in great leaps made by opening and shutting their shells very quickly. This is how they manage to escape their principal enemy, the starfish.

scallop

cockle

Cockles and Clams

These mollusks hide from their enemies in the sand. They move about by snapping open and shut their shells.

Razor Clams

Razor clams dig deep holes in the sand to hide from their enemies.

razor clam

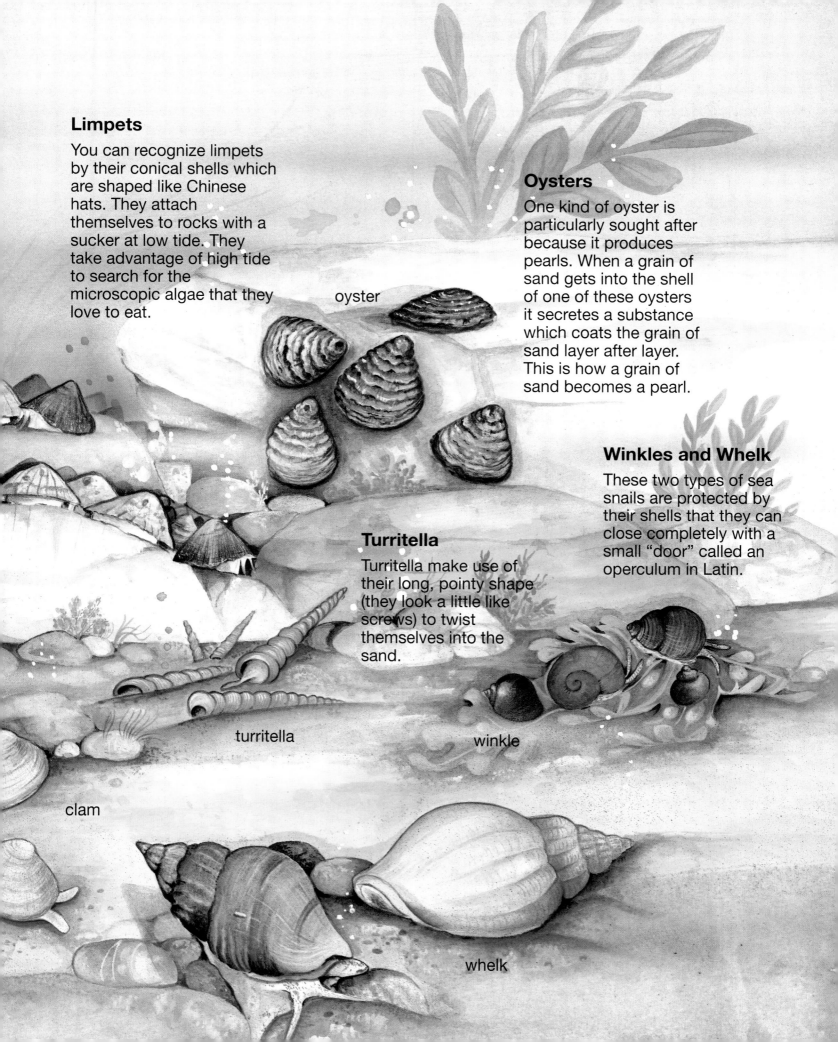

Limpets

You can recognize limpets by their conical shells which are shaped like Chinese hats. They attach themselves to rocks with a sucker at low tide. They take advantage of high tide to search for the microscopic algae that they love to eat.

oyster

Oysters

One kind of oyster is particularly sought after because it produces pearls. When a grain of sand gets into the shell of one of these oysters it secretes a substance which coats the grain of sand layer after layer. This is how a grain of sand becomes a pearl.

Winkles and Whelk

These two types of sea snails are protected by their shells that they can close completely with a small "door" called an operculum in Latin.

Turritella

Turritella make use of their long, pointy shape (they look a little like screws) to twist themselves into the sand.

turritella

winkle

clam

whelk

LEATHERBACK TURTLES

Leatherbacks are giant sea turtles with flexible carapaces. They can get as big as seven feet long and weigh more than 1,100 pounds. They are mostly found in warm waters. They used to be hunted for their meat and fat but are now a protected species. There are people in charge of watching over them when they come onto land to lay their eggs so that they don't get hurt while on the beach. Turtles do not have any teeth but they do have hooked beaks.

Leatherbacks sometimes travel several thousand miles in order to always return to the same beach to lay their eggs. Only the females leave the water.

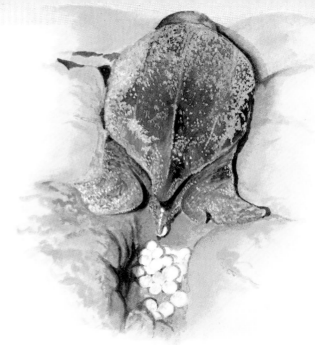

Only One Idea— Return to the Sea

Even though they are exhausted by laying their eggs the female leatherbacks do not rest. They go straight back to the sea; they use their front flippers like legs to pull themselves across the sand. It isn't easy to move those 1,100 pounds! Baby leatherbacks are also attracted to the sea as soon as they are born. Unfortunately, many dangers await the babies on the beach: crabs like to eat them and so do birds and large monitor lizards.

Female Leatherbacks Lay Eggs

The females dig deep holes in the sand with their back flippers and lay their eggs in the holes. They do not stay with their eggs but bury them in the sand and camouflage the hole. Then they return to the sea. The sun keeps the eggs warm and about two months later the baby leatherbacks break out of their eggs thanks to a small tooth that they each have on their snouts. Then they dig their way to the surface and the open air.

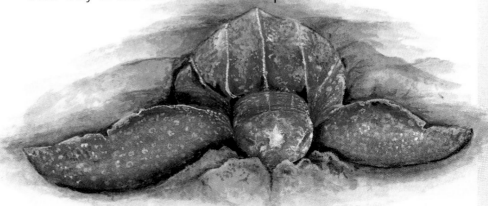

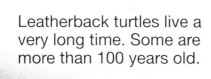

Leatherback turtles live a very long time. Some are more than 100 years old.

Trapped in the Mud

Sometimes leatherbacks lay eggs on mud-covered beaches. It is almost impossible for them to move forward. They sink into the mud little by little and weaken. If no one comes to help them they can die of exhaustion.

ISBN 2-215-06160-X